MISSION SAVE THE PLANET

THINGS YOU CAN DO TO HELP FIGHT GLOBAL WARMING

**SALLY RIDE &
TAM O'SHAUGHNESSY**

Illustrated by Andrew Arnold

Rb
Flash
Point

Sally Ride
Science

Roaring Brook Press
New York, NY

Sally Ride
Science

An innovative science content company.

Copyright © 2009 Sally Ride and Tam O'Shaughnessy
Illustrations copyright © 2009 by Andrew Arnold

Flash Point is an imprint of Roaring Brook Press, a division of
Holtzbrinck Publishing Holdings Limited Partnership.
175 Fifth Avenue, New York, New York 10010

Jacket and book design by Andrew Arnold

Cataloging-in-Publication Data is on file at the Library of Congress
ISBN-13: 978-1-59643-379-3   ISBN-10: 1-59643-379-5

Roaring Brook Press books are available for special promotions and premiums.
For details contact: Director of Special Markets, Holtzbrinck Publishers.

Printed on paper made of 40% post-consumer recycled content.

First Edition March 2009
1 2 3 4 5 6 7 8 9 10

Printed in February 2009 in the United States of America by Worzalla, Stevens Point,
Wisconsin

CONTENTS

CHAPTER 1

GLOBAL WARNING

When I was an astronaut, one of my favorite things to do was to float over to one of the small windows in the space shuttle and look down on Earth. From space, Earth's atmosphere looks like a fuzzy blue line ringing our planet—like someone took a blue crayon and drew a blue line all around it. But that thin blue band—our air—is Earth's space suit. It's all that protects us from the extreme conditions of space. It keeps us warm. It shields us from the Sun's harmful rays. It provides us with the oxygen we breathe. Without our atmosphere, life wouldn't be possible!

Yet over the past two centuries, people have been changing the atmosphere. We've been adding gases to the air that are making our planet warmer. This is changing Earth's climate. And, in one way or another, this is affecting our whole planet.

There are things you should know about Earth's changing climate—you can read all about these in Mission: Planet Earth. And there are things you can do—you can learn all about these in this book. So keep reading!

CHANGE THE AIR, CHANGE THE PLANET

Until relatively recently, people didn't have much of an effect on Earth. This is because there weren't many of us on the planet. In 1750, there were fewer than one billion people on our planet. Today, there are nearly *seven* billion of us. And every single one of us needs water, food, clothing, and shelter.

Humans are a very creative, caring, and resourceful species. As our population has grown sky high, we've developed agricultural methods to feed billions of people. We've built villages, towns, and cities to live in. We've crisscrossed the countryside with roads to transport food and other goods. We've made ships, cars, trains, and airplanes to travel in. We've invented technologies to light our cities, heat and cool our homes, and bring radio, telephone, television, and the Internet to people around the globe. But as we've advanced our civilization, we've used more and more and more energy.

Where does all of this energy come from? It comes from *fossil fuels*—oil, coal, and natural gas. For the past 200 years, these are the sources of energy we've come to depend on. The problem—and it's a whopper!—is that when fossil fuels are burned, they send *carbon dioxide* (CO_2) and other *greenhouse gases* into the air. Year after year for the past two centuries, carbon dioxide has been piling up in our atmosphere. And more is added every day. Carbon dioxide billows out of smokestacks and wafts out of tailpipes around the world—from Los Angeles and London to Moscow and Mumbai and from Beijing and Bangkok to Caracas and Khartoum.

The buildup of carbon dioxide is changing our air. And this is making our world warmer.

WEIGHING AIR

Take a deep breath. Feel the air rushing into your nose and lungs? It is so wispy and light that it seems weightless. But, of course, it isn't. We aren't aware that air has weight because we're surrounded by it—fish probably aren't aware that water has weight, either. The gases in the air around us can be weighed. Here's a simple experiment, so you can see for yourself.

First, get three balloons and a meter stick or yard stick. Tape an empty balloon to each end of the meter stick. Try to balance the meter stick on one finger. What happens to it? Now blow up the third balloon. Leave one of the original, deflated balloons on one end of the meter stick, and attach the blown-up balloon to the other end. Try to balance the meter stick on your finger again. What happens this time? Why?

1.

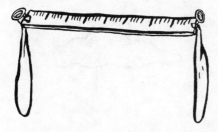

2.

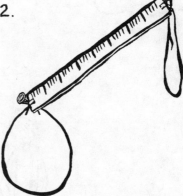

The side with the blown-up balloon is weighed down so the meter stick is no longer level. The only difference between these two balloons is that one is full of air!

EVEN MORE CO$_2$?

For the last few centuries, people have been cutting down trees all over the world. We use wood for fuel and lumber. We clear the land to build towns, grow food, and give animals a place to graze. About 90 percent of the forests that once grew in the United States have been cut down. About 20 percent of the Amazon rainforest has been cleared. Huge patches of tropical rainforest in Asia and South America are chopped down and burned every day. When trees are burned for fuel or to clear the land, carbon dioxide is released into the air. And with fewer trees around, less carbon dioxide is soaked up from the air for *photosynthesis*. So, deforestation is double trouble—it just adds to the problem of global climate warming.

FOSSIL FUELS

You've probably heard about fossil fuels. They come from the remains or "fossils" of prehistoric plants and animals that lived in swamps and oceans. Since all living things are based on carbon, their remains are mostly carbon, too. When these trees, algae, and small animals died, they decayed under layer after layer of sediments. They were buried deep inside Earth. Over millions and millions of years, intense pressure and heat cooked these fossils until only carbon and hydrogen were left—fossil fuels. And when fossil fuels are burned, the carbon is released into the air as carbon dioxide.

FOSSIL FUELISH

About 200 years ago, people started burning fossil fuels for energy. At first, it didn't seem like such a bad idea. A little bit releases a bunch of stored up energy when it's burned. For instance, burning a pound of coal produces a lot more energy than burning a pound of wood. So the idea really caught on.

But like burning wood in a campfire, burning fossil fuels sends carbon dioxide and other *greenhouse gases* into the air. This made scientists worry. They knew the gases wouldn't just disappear . . . instead, they'd pile up in the air.

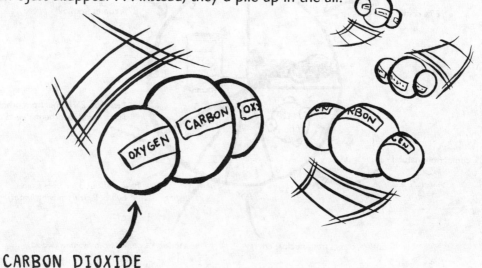

CARBON DIOXIDE

HOW DO WE USE ENERGY TODAY?

Everything we do takes energy—including driving cars, lighting homes, and making things in factories. Here's how it breaks down across the globe.

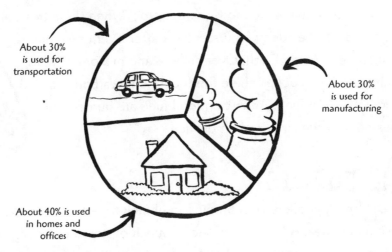

About 30% is used for transportation

About 30% is used for manufacturing

About 40% is used in homes and offices

WHERE DOES OUR ENERGY COME FROM?

About 85 percent of the energy the world consumes comes from fossil fuels . . .

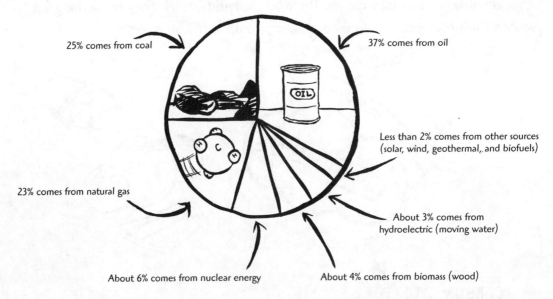

25% comes from coal

37% comes from oil

Less than 2% comes from other sources (solar, wind, geothermal, and biofuels)

23% comes from natural gas

About 3% comes from hydroelectric (moving water)

About 6% comes from nuclear energy

About 4% comes from biomass (wood)

Here are some of the ways we use fossil fuels today.

OIL is turned into

- gasoline for cars, diesel fuel for trucks, and jet fuel for airplanes;
- fertilizers for farms and backyards;
- synthetic fabrics for clothes and carpets; and
- plastic for bottles, toothbrushes, guitar strings—you name it!

COAL is burned in power plants to make electricity.

NATURAL GAS is piped into homes to heat and cool them.

And, yes, each time we refine or burn these fuels or make products from them, carbon dioxide is added to the air.

4 U 2 Do

Be an electricity sleuth. Find out how the electricity that flows into your home is generated. How much is produced by coal or other nonrenewable fossil fuels? How much is made by energy sources like solar energy, wind power, and other renewable energy sources? Start your investigation by going online to your local electricity provider or by calling them.

EARTH, THE GREENHOUSE

Earth's atmosphere is like a greenhouse—it lets sunshine in but doesn't let much heat out. This *greenhouse effect* is a natural process that warms Earth. Here's how it works. As sunlight falls on the oceans and lands, it is absorbed at the surface and warms our planet. The warm water and ground cool down by radiating the heat away. Most of the gases in our air, like oxygen and nitrogen, let the heat pass through. But a few gases—called greenhouse gases—such as carbon dioxide and water trap some of the heat before it seeps into space. They make our planet a pleasant place to live. If there were no heat-trapping gases in our air, Earth would be a cold, desert world much like our Moon. So the natural greenhouse effect is a good thing.

What's happening today as people send ever more greenhouse gases into the air? The greenhouse effect is getting stronger and stronger and our planet is getting warmer and warmer. This human-magnified greenhouse effect—definitely *not* a good thing!

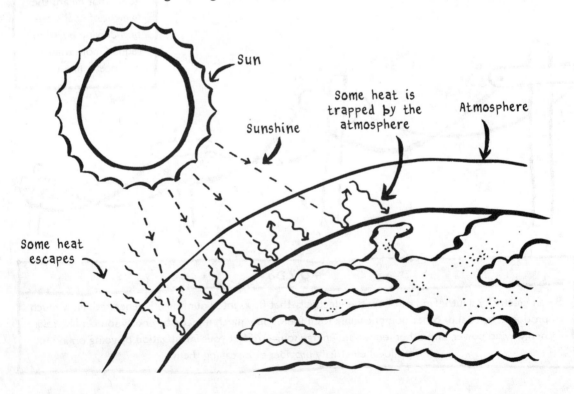

Sun

Sunshine

Some heat is trapped by the atmosphere

Atmosphere

Some heat escapes

TOO MUCH CO$_2$

Once we began burning fossil fuels for energy, we started adding carbon dioxide to our air. Burning coal, burning oil, and burning natural gas send tons and tons of carbon dioxide into our air. How much? So far, we've added 26 billion metric tons. And every day we add more.

For a long time, no one knew how much carbon dioxide was in the atmosphere. Then in 1958, a young scientist named Charles Keeling set up a monitoring station near the top of Mauna Loa, the biggest volcano in Hawaii. He measured the amount of carbon dioxide in the air continuously for many years. His graph, called the Keeling Curve, is one of the most famous graphs in science. Today, monitoring stations all over the world still record these measurements.

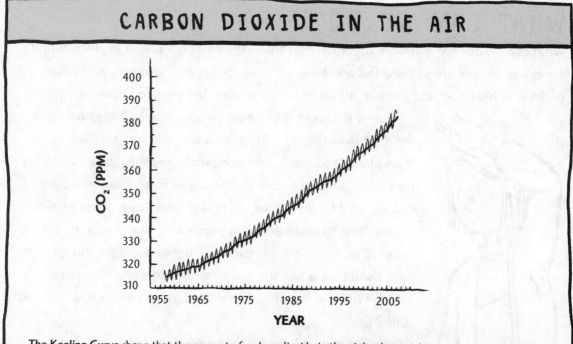

CARBON DIOXIDE IN THE AIR

The Keeling Curve shows that the amount of carbon dioxide in the air has been going up every year. In 1958, there were about 315 molecules of carbon dioxide out of every one million molecules of air (called parts per million or ppm). Today there are about 385 ppm of carbon dioxide! That's a mega increase in just 50 years.

TEMPERATURES RISING

As carbon dioxide builds up in the air, it magnifies the greenhouse effect. This means our world is getting warmer. In the last century, Earth's average temperature has risen about 1.5°F. This may not sound like very much, but it is. Already scientists have measured changes all over the globe. Oceans are warmer. Mountain glaciers are melting. Ice shelves are crumbling into the sea. Sea levels are rising. Weather patterns are different. And from the rainforests and dry deserts to the icy poles and salty seas, animals and plants are struggling to beat the heat.

WHAT CAN WE DO?

What can we do? We can work together. And that's just what people all over the world are doing. People are working fast and furiously to come up with solutions to stop the buildup of heat-trapping gases in our air. We need energy, but we need to use energy

sources that emit little or no carbon dioxide. The good news is that they already exist—as sunshine, wind, water, fuels made from plants, and more. And people all over the globe are already using them. Once we scale up the use of these clean-energy sources, we'll be on our way to taking better care of our planet.

Switching to clean energy is important. But there's something more *all* of us can do. We can do it right now, right this minute and it will take a big bite out of global warming. Conserve energy! Just use less of it. This is the fastest, cheapest, and easiest thing to do.

You've probably heard the expression "go green." It means living in a way that lessens our impact on Earth. In the next chapters you'll find ideas to help you live a greener life.

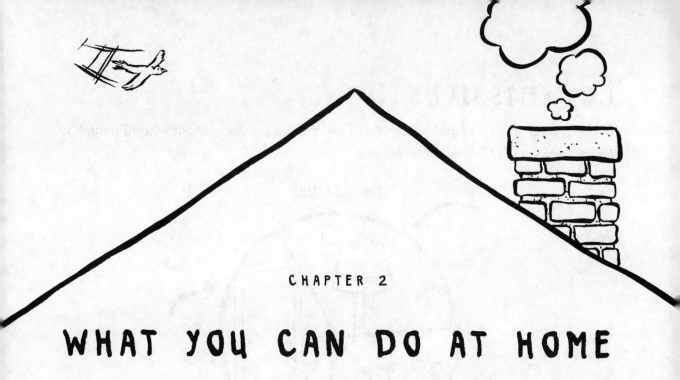

CHAPTER 2

WHAT YOU CAN DO AT HOME

SWITCH. CONSERVE.
MAKE SOME NOISE.

Nearly everything we do uses energy—from flipping on lights, watching TV, and riding in cars to microwaving snacks, playing video games, and washing clothes. Most of these activities use electricity. Electricity is made in power plants by burning fossil fuels, such as coal. When electricity is generated this way—up goes CO_2 into the air. When you ride in a car, gasoline is burned in the engine—up goes CO_2 into the air. When factories make the things you buy, like jeans or cell phones, the machines are powered with fossil fuels—up goes CO_2 into the air.

When you use less energy, less fossil fuel is burned and less CO_2 goes into the air. It's as simple as that!

CO$_2$ EMISSIONS

In the United States a typical household of two people produces about 60,000 pounds of carbon dioxide (CO$_2$) emissions every year.

ENERGY USE

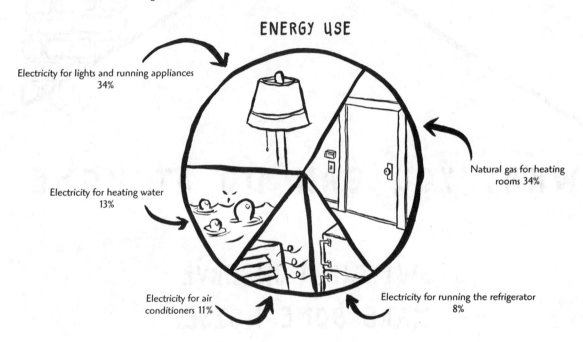

Electricity for lights and running appliances 34%

Natural gas for heating rooms 34%

Electricity for heating water 13%

Electricity for air conditioners 11%

Electricity for running the refrigerator 8%

LET THE SUN SHINE, LET THE WIND BLOW

You've probably heard the phrases "clean energy" and *renewable energy.*" What do they mean? Clean energy usually means electricity that is generated without producing pollution (like carbon dioxide). How is this done? By using wind, water, sunshine, or some other nonpolluting source of energy to generate the electricity that lights your home and runs your refrigerator. These energy sources are also called renewable energy because it's impossible to use them up. Let the Sun shine on rows of solar panels and generate electricity for a nearby town. When the Sun comes up the next day, do it again!

FACT FINDING MISSION . . . YOUR HOME

Knowledge is power. The first step toward living the green life is to know how you and your family live today. Ask a parent or older sister or brother to take this *We're Going Green Survey* with you and find out.

WE'RE GOING GREEN SURVEY

How many people live in your home? _____

HOME HEATING AND ELECTRICITY

How does your family heat your home?

- ☐ Natural gas
- ☐ Electric heat
- ☐ Oil
- ☐ Other

What is your family's average monthly gas bill? _____

What is your family's average monthly fuel oil bill? _____

What is your family's average monthly electric bill? _____

How is the electricity generated for your home? What percentage is generated by . . .
  coal or other nonrenewable energy sources? _____
  solar energy, wind power, or other renewable energy sources? _____

What temperature is your thermostat set to in winter?
  During the daytime _____
  During the nighttime _____

Does your family use air conditioners during the summer?   ☐ Yes   ☐ No

What is your air conditioner set to during the daytime? _____

What is your air conditioner set to during the nighttime? _____

Does your family home have central air conditioning? ☐ Yes ☐ No

Which kind of light bulbs does your family use?
☐ standard light bulbs ☐ compact fluorescent light bulbs

Where does the water for your home come from?
☐ well ☐ community water system ☐ other source(s)

RECYCLING

Does your family recycle? ☐ Yes ☐ No

If so, what?
☐ plastic ☐ newspapers and other paper products
☐ glass ☐ aluminum and steel cans

TRANSPORTATION

How many cars does your family own? _____

What is the average gas mileage for each car (miles per gallon or mpg)? _____

How many miles does your family put on your car(s)?
per week _____ or per year _____

How many people in your family carpool?
to school _____ or to work _____

How many members of your family use public transportation? _____

WHAT'S YOUR CARBON FOOTPRINT?

Now you know a lot about how you and your family live today. And you know that every time you watch TV, flip on a light, or guzzle a bottle of water, you're adding carbon dioxide to the air. To find out just how much, calculate your *carbon footprint*. This will tell you how much carbon goes into the air (as CO_2) from all the energy that you use. And get this: The average person living in the United States has a carbon footprint of about 30,000 pounds of carbon each year. That's 15 tons of carbon—more than two fully-grown African elephants weigh. Gather your *We're Going Green Survey*. Then ask a parent, or older brother or sister, to help you find a Web site with a carbon calculator, so you can calculate your family's carbon footprint.

Once you know your family's carbon footprint, it's time to make it smaller. There are lots of things you can do at home that will make a difference—they'll shrink your footprint and save money!

Wow, look at the size of that footprint!

AROUND THE HOUSE...

Heating and cooling are responsible for a big chunk of the energy your house uses. How you prepare for hot and cold days can make a real difference to your carbon footprint.

USE GREEN POWER

More and more power companies are generating some electricity from clean-energy sources instead of producing all of their electricity from polluting fossil fuels. They've added solar energy, wind power, and biofuels made from plants. These clean fuels emit little or no carbon dioxide. Some of your electricity can come from green power, too.

Talk to your parents about looking into their utility company's green-energy options. Most power companies allow you to purchase some of your electricity from solar energy, wind power, and other clean energies.

4 U 2 Do

For one day, keep track of all the things you do that use energy—and, as a result, send carbon dioxide into the air. Some activities to include: watching TV, listening to music, turning on lights, riding in a car, checking e-mail, and so on. Doing this for even one day will make you more aware of your energy consumption. Share the results with your family or friends and get them thinking about living the green life, too.

UMMMMM . . .

Would you wear shorts and a T-shirt outside on a cold winter day? Probably not. Then why wear them inside? Pull on a sweatshirt and a pair of socks instead of turning up the heat.

SMALL THING, BIG DIFFERENCE

During the winter, make it a habit to open the curtains or blinds during day to let the sunshine warm your house. Just remember to close them at night to stop heat from escaping.

A MATTER OF DEGREES

Talk to your parents about lowering the furnace thermostat 2°F in the winter. This will cut energy use by 1 percent.

CO₂ & U If you lower your furnace thermostat in the winter by 2°F, you'll prevent more than 350 pounds of carbon dioxide from going into the air each year.

SEAL IT

Drafty windows and doors let the great outdoors in. They make it harder to keep your house warm in the winter (and think about all those crawly things that get in). Seal up the leaks in your house.

Talk to your parents about sealing leaky windows and putting weather strips around drafty doorframes. Homes that are well sealed use less energy because furnaces and fans don't have to work so hard. Less energy used = More $$ saved!

CO₂ & U If you seal leaky doors and windows, you'll prevent more than 600 pounds of carbon dioxide from going into the air each year.

SUMMER BREEZE

In the summer, there are things you can do to stay cool besides turning on the air conditioner. Open some windows and let in the breeze.

MAKE SOME NOISE!

Talk to your parents about using the air conditioner less or not at all. Ceiling and window fans move the air and can make a room feel up to 7 °F cooler. And fans use far less electricity than air conditioners. That means they save money.

KEEP IT COOL

Dress in cool clothes—light fabrics in light colors (light colors reflect sunlight; dark colors absorb sunlight, making you even warmer).

A BRIGHT IDEA

Talk to your parents about replacing conventional light bulbs with compact fluorescent (CFL) bulbs. Replacing just one 60-watt light bulb will save about $7.50 a year—more than the cost of the fluorescent bulb.

A compact fluorescent light bulb uses 75 percent less energy than a regular light bulb. Saving energy and money—that's a bright idea!

If you replace five regular light bulbs with compact fluorescents, you'll prevent 500 pounds of carbon dioxide from going into the air each year.

AN OPEN-AND-SHUT CASE

During the summer, keep the curtains or blinds closed during the day to keep out the Sun's heat. Then open them at night to let in the cooler night air.

LIGHTS OUT

Not just at bedtime! Turn off the lights when you're not using them. That doesn't mean you have to sit in the dark or use candles. It just means using lights only when you need them.

4 U 2 Do

If you're reading this book at home, set it down for a minute and take a stroll. Are there lights on in any empty rooms? If there are . . . you know what to do!

COMMON GOOD

Talk to your parents about speaking with your landlord, homeowner's association, co-op committee, or condo association about practicing conservation measures in common areas. One great suggestion is to ask them to replace conventional light bulbs with long-lasting, energy-saving compact flourescent bulbs in hallways, stairwells, and other communal areas.

By the way . . .

What's a watt? It's a measure of how much energy that light bulb you flipped on uses each second. Since a watt is just a teeny bit of energy, it's more common to hear about kilowatts. One kilowatt is equal to 1,000 watts. When your parents get the electric bill, they get charged by the kilowatt-hour. If a 100-watt light bulb is left burning for 10 hours, it will consume one kilowatt-hour of electricity. So, if you want to kill-a-watt, turn the lights out when no one's using them!

4 U 2 Do—Do the Write Thing

You may be too young to vote. But you can still make your voice heard in government. Write to your representative and let her or him know how Earth's changing climate concerns you. Are the folks on Capitol Hill tuned in to climate change? Write a letter to your senator or congressperson to find out.

Tell him or her how you feel about climate change and ask what Congress is doing to address the problems we face. Let them know you hope they support recycling, the development of clean energies, and fuel-efficient cars. You may be surprised to know that members of Congress pay attention to their mail. That's how they find out how people in their district feel about the issues that concern them.

Here are some tips for writing a great letter to your senator or congressperson.

- Make sure to use the person's name and title, such as "Dear Senator Brown:"

- Short letters are fine.

- Use your own words!

- Be specific. Mention things you are interested in, like climate change, solar energy, or recycling.

- Bring up examples from your town, such as a great recycling program.

You can find the names and addresses of your representatives here: http://www.house.gov/house/MemberWWW_by_State.shtml
And senators here:
http://www.senate.gov/general/contact_information/senators_cfm.cfm

IN THE KITCHEN...

THINK SMALL

Use the microwave, toaster oven, or slow cooker whenever you can. Smaller spaces heat up faster. That means it takes less energy to heat them. An average microwave uses only 20 percent of the energy that a regular oven uses to cook the same food. So, toss your grilled-cheese sandwich into the toaster oven and reheat your leftovers in the microwave.

DRIP, DROP, DRY

Is it your turn to do the dishes? The good news is that most dishwashers are more energy and water efficient than washing dishes by hand. In fact, running a dishwasher uses about one-half the energy and one-sixth the water. You can save energy by running the dishwasher only with a full load. And if you want to save even more energy, turn off the "heated dry" cycle and let the dishes drip dry.

A WATCHED COOKIE DOESN'T BAKE

Sure, it's hard not to peek at chocolate chip cookies as they're baking. But each time you open the oven door, the temperature drops 25–75°F. Not only does this waste energy, but your cookies will take longer to bake.

A LITTLE DOES A LOT

Talk to your parents about setting the refrigerator and the freezer at the lowest possible settings that will keep food safe. In general, food keeps in the fridge at 37°–42°F and in the freezer at 0°–5°F. Check the owner's manual for your refrigerator to see what temperatures are recommended.

BE AN ENERGY STAR

When it's time for your family to buy a new refrigerator or other appliance, tell them to look for the Energy Star® label. It means the product is energy efficient. For example, today's Energy Star® refrigerators use one-half the electricity and emit one-half the carbon dioxide of older models. *Energy efficiency* = Cleaner air and a healthier planet.

4 U 2 Do

Make a list of what's in the refrigerator and hang it on the door. Now you can decide what you want *before* opening the door. And as the fridge empties, you've got a grocery list all ready to go.

WHO LET THE (COLD) AIR OUT?

Every time you open the refrigerator door, out comes the cold air. If you stand in front of the fridge with the door open for five minutes deciding what kind of juice you want, you'll let out 30 percent of the cold air. That's a lot of wasted electricity.

4 U 2 DO Peek inside your freezer. Is there a lot of empty space? Here's a simple freezer fix: Find an empty plastic jug. Fill the jug about two-thirds full of water and put it in the freezer. A full freezer stays colder. This reduces the amount of electricity it needs to run. Just remember not to fill the jug too full—water expands when it freezes and the jug could burst inside your freezer.

WASTE NOT

How much do you (and every other person) throw away each day? Almost 4.6 pounds of waste! All that stuff—water bottles, food wrappers, newspapers, and cans—overloads landfills. What to do? Recycle and reduce the amount of stuff you buy.

By the Way . . .

Americans guzzle more than 70 million plastic bottles of water a day. Each bottle takes hundreds of years to decompose in a landfill. But even worse, turning oil into plastic to make the bottles releases gobs of carbon dioxide into the air. Next time you're thirsty, grab a glass!

GREEN MEANS MORE THAN LETTUCE

Talk to your parents about being green consumers. This means buying in bulk, consuming less, and choosing products that are made of recycled materials. It also means buying products that can be reused or recycled. As a family, think about how much you really need to live well *and* live in an environmentally friendly way.

CO_2 & U   If you buy products with less packaging and in containers made from recycled material, you'll prevent more than 200 pounds of carbon dioxide from going into the air each year.

AT THE DINNER TABLE...

THINK GLOBALLY, BUY LOCALLY

You've heard about carnivores, herbivores, and omnivores. But what about *locavores*? A locavore is someone who eats locally grown food. This usually means buying food that has been produced within 100 miles of your neighborhood. Why buy local? Because getting food from farm to market—by truck, train, ship, or airplane—uses a lot of energy.

BUY CLOSE TO HOME

Talk to your parents about looking for locally grown food in your supermarket and shopping at local farmers' markets.

4 U 2 Do—Start a Vegetable Garden

There's no produce more local than the stuff you grow yourself! You don't have to have a big backyard to grow veggies such as tomatoes—you can grow them in a container on your deck, patio, or small porch. You can even grow herbs from seeds or young plants in small containers on a windowsill. Try these pasta and pizza herbs: basil, parsley, and oregano. Or try these herbs for tea: lemon balm, peppermint, and chamomile. Here's how.

STARTING FROM SEEDS
Fill a small, shallow container with seed-starting mix. Read the seed packet for planting depth. Place a light 3 to 6 inches above the container and keep the mix evenly moist until your seeds begin to sprout. When the mix dries out, water the seedlings completely with a spray bottle. If you want to move your plants outside, they need to adjust to being outdoors. Place them outside for a few hours each day, increasing to a full day by the end of a week.

STARTING FROM PLANTS
You can purchase many young herb plants from local farmers' markets, grocery stores, or nurseries. Keep them in the container they come in or transplant them to a garden or another container with good drainage. The Sun will do its part, you just need to remember to water!

4 U 2 Do—How Far Has Your Meal Traveled?

On average, food in the United States travels 1,490 miles to get to your plate. That means food is a real gas guzzler. Transporting produce and meat for thousands of miles means tons of extra carbon dioxide spewed into the air. How far did your dinner travel to your table? The answer may surprise you.

At the supermarket, try to investigate where your food comes from. Think back on a recent dinner at home and fill in the chart. Pick three or four menu items from the meal. Then, at your local grocery store, take a whirlwind world tour of where your food came from. If the food is prepackaged, use the packaging location. For fruits and vegetables, check the produce signs or ask the produce manager.

Compare mileage "scores" for each item on your dinner menu. What foods traveled farthest? What was different about the lowest and highest scoring foods?

HOW FAR HAS YOUR MEAL TRAVELED?

MENU	DINNER ITEM	WHERE FROM	MILES FROM HOME
Meat			
Seafood			
Poultry			
Vegetable			
Pasta/Rice			
Fruit			
Dessert			
Drink			
Other		TOTAL MILES =	

IN THE BEDROOM...

WATCH OUT FOR PHANTOMS

Your DVD player, TV, computer, and other electronics might not be on right now but they're still sucking energy. The electricity used when appliances and electronics are connected to power outlets is called the phantom load. These phantoms steal energy and money when you're not looking. What's the solution? Unplug your TV, computer, and toaster when you're not using them or use a power strip to shut them down.

POWER DOWN

Talk to your parents about buying some power strips to connect appliances (all except the refrigerator!) and electronics. Once you hook up the energy phantoms to power strips you can just flip off the power strips and start saving precious energy and money.

4 U 2 Do

An easy way to spot your energy phantoms at work is to turn off the lights. Walk around your bedroom, kitchen, and living room and chances are you'll see digital read-outs glowing all around you. Anywhere you see a tiny red, yellow, or green light, you're seeing a phantom at work, sucking electricity to keep the light glowing.

TREE - FREE

Get this: Making recycled paper instead of making paper from new trees, consumes 65 percent less energy, uses 80 percent less water, and sends 95 percent less carbon dioxide into the air.

LESS IS MORE

If your family recycles paper products, that's great. If your family buys recycled paper for school and home, that's *really* great. But if you want to do even more, come up with a plan to *use less* paper. Buy products with less paper packaging. Use a small chalkboard or erasable whiteboard to jot down notes. Use old-fashioned kitchen towels instead of paper towels. Cancel subscriptions to magazines no one's reading.

"PAPER OR PLASTIC?"

You've probably been asked this question at your local supermarket. Plastic bags can hang around in landfills for hundreds of years, and paper bags often mean cutting down precious trees to make them. So what's the answer? Bring your own bag—a reusable canvas or cloth bag is the best way to help the environment.

4 U 2 Do

Your family probably recycles already. But it's easy to forget what can and what can't be recycled. Most recycling programs mail out a chart with all the do's and don'ts. If you don't have one, give them a call. Stick the chart on the fridge. Now play the recycle game. See how much less trash you can accumulate each week.

IN THE BATHROOM...

SLOW THE FLOW

What's the biggest energy sapper in the bathroom? The tub and shower. Sure, you need to stay clean. But the hot water you use every day when you bathe can add up to a lot of wasted water and energy to heat it. You've probably heard that taking a shower wastes less water than taking a bath. The truth is it depends on how long a shower you take and what kind of showerhead you have.

If you have an older showerhead, you could be using as much as five gallons of water a minute. Most bathtubs hold about 50 gallons of water. So if you take a ten-minute shower using five gallons of water a minute, how much water would you use? Do the math. You would use just as much hot water as you would if you took a bath. Of course taking shorter showers helps.

GO WITH THE LOW FLOW

Talk to your parents about purchasing low-flow showerheads. They're relatively cheap to buy. The money spent will be made back many times over in the money saved by heating less water. Low-flow showerheads release only about 2.5 gallons of water a minute. Now do the math again. If you took a ten-minute shower, how much water would you save?

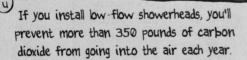

If you install low-flow showerheads, you'll prevent more than 350 pounds of carbon dioxide from going into the air each year.

4 U 2 Do

Ask your parent or older sister or brother to help you take the top off the toilet. Add a few drops of blue (any color will do) food color to the tank. Make sure no one uses the toilet for about 15 minutes. Then check. If the blue color shows up in the toilet bowl, it's leaking. Congratulations! You're a water-leak wizard!

NO RUNNING ALLOWED

It takes energy for community water systems to purify and pipe the water that comes into your home. So don't let the water run when you're brushing your teeth or washing your hands.

4 U 2 Do

Challenge your family to take shorter showers. Use a stopwatch, regular watch, or egg timer to keep track of how fast everyone showers. After each person showers, they can jot down how long it took him or her on a scorecard where everyone can see it. At the end of the week, the person with the shortest shower takes the prize. What she or he wins is up to you!

IN THE GARAGE...

GOOD-BYE GAS HOG?

If someone in your family is thinking of getting a new car, help them research fuel-efficient cars. Each gallon of gasoline saved keeps 20 pounds of carbon dioxide out of the air.

LIGHTEN THE LOAD

Talk to your parents about keeping the car trunk as empty as possible. The lighter the ride, the better mpg it will get.

CO₂ & U If you keep the car tires properly inflated, you'll prevent 250 pounds of carbon dioxide from going into the air each year. Why? Tires that are low on air burn more gas.

How far do you like to walk or bike? Talk to your parents about all the places—school, store, park, friends' homes—you can walk or ride your bike to. Then set a distance that's comfortable for you and make a pact with yourself: Anytime you have to travel that distance (or less) get there under your own power—shoe it! If you aren't sure how far away your destination is, you can figure it out using an online pedometer. You can find one at www.gmap-pedometer.com.

HOP ON A BUS OR BIKE

Talk to your family about saving gas by not driving the car two days a week. Check out public transportation in your community, start your own *carpools*, or hop on your bike or walk—your whole family can get some exercise and take care of the environment at the same time.

CO₂ & U

If your family doesn't drive a car two days each week, it would keep more than 1,500 pounds of carbon dioxide from going into the air in a year.

Lots of cities around the world—from Washington, D.C. to London to Beijing—are declaring car-free days. People who live in these cities, or who travel in and out of them each day, are encouraged to leave their cars at home. How do they get around? By bus, bicycle, ferry, scooter, shuttle, subway, or taxi-bike—or by just walking to where they're going.

IN THE LAUNDRY ...

GOOD DRIP . . .
Air-drying clothes on a clothesline saves energy and money.

. . . BAD DRIP
A single leaky faucet can waste a whopping 2,000 gallons of water in a year. Go on drip patrol. Check out all the faucets in your home. Then talk to your parents about fixing any leaks.

By the way . . .

The average American uses 80 to 100 gallons of water at home each day.

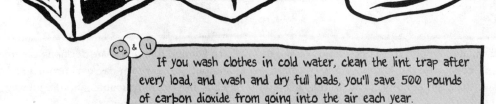

If you wash clothes in cold water, clean the lint trap after every load, and wash and dry full loads, you'll save 500 pounds of carbon dioxide from going into the air each year.

WASH AND DRY

Okay, your socks and underwear need to be washed every time you wear them. But what about those jeans you wore to school yesterday? Are they *really* dirty? Washers and dryers eat up lots of energy. Washing clothes in cold water helps—and clothes get just as clean. Only washing and drying full loads helps, too.

CO₂ & U

Is it time for your family to get a new hot-water heater? If the old one is replaced with an energy-efficient model, you'll prevent more than 3,000 pounds of carbon dioxide from going into the air each year. Your family will save about $250 in energy costs each year, too.

LOOK OUT FOR LINT

If you need to use the dryer, clean the lint filter after every load. This improves airflow and energy efficiency.

TRASH

IN THE YARD . . .

PLANT A TREE!

Trees are good for the environment. They soak up lots of carbon dioxide gas during photosynthesis. As trees grow, they fight global warming by removing carbon dioxide from the air and storing it in their leaves, branches, and trunk. And, that's not all. A well-placed tree can shade your home in the summer and lower your cooling bills.

Talk to your parents about planting a tree in your yard or—if you live in a city—calling the parks department to plant a street tree on your block.

4 U 2 Do

Next time you hear thunder, don't be annoyed if your soccer game is rained out. Use the time to build your own rainwater catch instead—all you need is a new trash barrel with a lid. "New" is important so the water you collect will be as clean as possible. Talk to your parents about finding a good place to put your rain barrel—maybe under a downspout or gutter. Now you're ready to catch some rain. When the sky clears, put the lid on your rain barrel to keep out insects and debris. The rainwater you catch is perfect for watering your plants—indoors and out.

CO_2 & U

If you plant a tree, you can save 50 pounds of carbon dioxide from going into the air each year.

CATCH A FALLING . . .

. . . raindrop! Catch the rain and collect it in a bucket or a basin. Use it to water your houseplants. Remember—conserving water conserves energy.

If you have a yard, use your own muscle power to push a reel mower, instead of using a lawn mower that guzzles gasoline. That will prevent 80 pounds of carbon dioxide from going into the air each year.

By the Way . . .

Don't bother with the grass clippings. Instead of bagging them, leave them on the lawn. Insects, microbes, and worms will decompose the cut grass, adding organic matter to the soil. No fertilizer needed. Let your lawn feed itself.

4 U 2 Do

Where do all the lawn clippings and veggie leftovers go at your house? Instead of tossing them, turn them into organic mulch for your plants. Compost is one of nature's best soil additions.

Get some wood or cinder blocks about 3 feet high and make a three-sided bin. Leave the fourth side open for turning the mulch. Your compost bin needs the right ratio of browns, like dried leaves, and greens, like grass clippings and kitchen scraps, such as discarded veggies and coffee grinds. The ideal ratio is about 25 parts brown to 1 part green. Start layering the browns and greens. Now let the microbes munch. Turn the pile over every so often to speed up the decomposition. It will take about one year for the bottom material to be ready, so the sooner you get started the sooner you'll be using your own homemade compost!

NO MORE BIG FOOT!

After you and your family make the changes you want to live a greener life, calculate your carbon footprint again. You may be surprised by how much you've reduced your footprint and energy bills, too. Your family will thank you today. Your planet will thank you tomorrow.

CHAPTER 3

WHAT YOU CAN DO AT SCHOOL

YOUR TURN...TO TEACH!

At school you can make wise choices about how you use energy, too. And you can encourage your friends and teachers to do the same. Just remember . . . *switch* to clean energy, *conserve* energy, and *make some noise* apply just as much at school as they do at home.

Sure, your teachers are there to teach you the 3 **R**s (**R**eading, w**R**iting, and a**R**ithmetic) plus science, history, and much more. But you are an important member of the teaching team, too. Your teachers count on you to listen and learn with your eyes, ears, and mind wide open. But they also count on learning from you—with your voice, hands, and heart wide open. So don't be shy about sharing what you know about making your school a greener place to learn—it's your turn to teach!

GREEN UP!

Schools across the country are going green. Some schools are soaking up the sun with their own solar panels, some are harnessing the wind with their own wind turbines, some are conserving energy and water every which way they can, and some lucky schools are brand new or have been refurbished with the latest green materials and energy efficient technologies. And get this: Many of these schools received grant money to go green—*sweet!*

Talk to your teacher or principal about checking with your state's Department of Education, Department of Energy, and Environmental Protection Agency, as well as local high-tech and utility companies and local and state foundations, to find out what green schools grant programs they have available and if your school is eligible to apply.

WASTE-FREE LUNCH DAYS

When you bring your lunch to school, do you use a lunch box instead of a paper bag? Pack food in reusable containers. Use a thermos or other reusable container for your drink. Purchase snacks in bulk to save on extra packaging. Better yet, try a piece of fresh fruit—it comes in its own packaging.

By the Way . . .

The average student tosses more than 65 pounds of food packaging each school year.
That's probably more than your dog weighs . . . woof!

GAMES ON THE GREEN

Do you and your friends like sports or music? Next time you're at a concert or game, look around and see if you can spot the signs of a green event. The promoters will be proud they're Earth-friendly, so they'll make sure you notice! And if you can't tell the event is trying to reduce its environmental footprint, it probably means it isn't. You know what to look for . . . posters saying renewable energy is powering the event, vendors serving food and drinks in paper and cardboard food containers instead of polystyrene ones, and *recycling* bins everywhere.

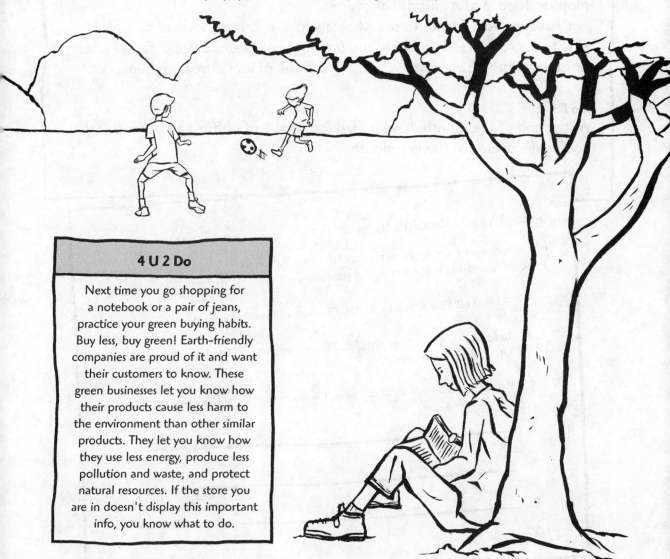

4 U 2 Do

Next time you go shopping for a notebook or a pair of jeans, practice your green buying habits. Buy less, buy green! Earth-friendly companies are proud of it and want their customers to know. These green businesses let you know how their products cause less harm to the environment than other similar products. They let you know how they use less energy, produce less pollution and waste, and protect natural resources. If the store you are in doesn't display this important info, you know what to do.

4 U 2 Do—Nothing New at School

Lots of energy goes into manufacturing new products. So lots of carbon dioxide is added to the air when new things are made. Think you could go without buying anything new for a week or a month (except essential school supplies, food, and medicine, of course)?

Challenge your friends to see who can go the longest. Instead of buying new things (clothes, CDs, DVDs), try scouting out neighborhood garage sales or have a clothes swap with your friends. Think of it as a treasure hunt.

Go For It
At the end of the month, have a "fashion show" of outfits and other things you've discovered in the last month.

School Year's Resolution

Resolutions aren't just for New Year's. Make a resolution to go green at school. Here are some ideas and some room to add your own.

- When I take my lunch to school, I'll make it a waste-free one.

- Before I buy new school supplies, I'll scrounge around the house to see what's left over from last year.

- Before I grab a fresh sheet of paper, I'll use both sides of the sheet I'm using.

- _____

- _____

- _____

HOW GREEN IS YOUR SCHOOL?

Make some noise! Talk to your teacher or school principal about forming a green team to investigate how green your school is. Students, teachers, and administrators can be part of the team. What's their assignment? To go on a fact-finding mission to find out the environmental impact of the school and where the school is wasting energy—and money. They'll check out the classrooms and bathrooms, the cafeteria and library, the auditorium and main office, the gym and playground, and the bus and car drop-off zone.

_____ SCHOOL IS GOING GREEN SURVEY

WHOLE SCHOOL

What are the annual energy costs of your school? Don't forget to include snack bars, athletic fields, storage sheds, and outdoor lighting.

Electricity _____
Heating _____
Water heating _____
Air-conditioning _____

Does your school pay for other energy costs?

Transportation _____   Other _____   Outdoor lighting _____

ELECTRICITY

How is the electricity generated for your school? The team can find out by going online to the school's local electricity provider or by calling them. What percentage is generated by . . .

coal or other nonrenewable energy sources?   _____

solar energy, wind power, or other renewable energy sources?   _____

HEATING AND COOLING

What fuel is used to heat your school?

☐ Natural gas   ☐ Oil
☐ Electric heat   ☐ Other

Does the heating system have a thermostat that can be programmed?   Yes ☐   No ☐

What temperature is the thermostat set to in winter?

Daytime _____ Nighttime _____

What setting is the thermostat set to in summer?

Daytime _____ Nighttime _____

Does your school have central air conditioning? ☐ Yes ☐ No

WATER

Where does the water for your school come from?

☐ A well ☐ A community water system ☐ Other source(s)

How many water heaters does your school have?

☐ 1 ☐ 2 ☐ Other

What is the temperature setting on the water heater(s)? _____

Are the water pipes and water heaters insulated? ☐ Yes ☐ No

RECYCLING

Does your school recycle? ☐ Yes ☐ No

Where are the recycling bins located?

☐ Classrooms ☐ Hallways
☐ Cafeteria ☐ Outside areas

What does your school recycle?

☐ Glass ☐ Newspaper / paper products
☐ Plastic ☐ Print cartridges
☐ Computers ☐ Aluminum and steel cans

Does your school collect gray water (water that is lightly used)? ☐ Yes ☐ No

If yes, what is it used for? ☐ Watering the landscaping ☐ Other

CAFETERIA

Where does the food served in the cafeteria come from?

Is it sourced from local farms and producers?   ☐ Yes   ☐ No

Is it trucked to the local cafeteria food distributor from hundreds or thousands of miles away?   ☐ Yes   ☐ No

SCHOOL YARD/SCHOOL GROUNDS

Is your school landscaped with native plants (plants that are adapted to your local climate)?
☐ Yes   ☐ No

Are trees planted around school buildings?   ☐ Yes   ☐ No

TRANSPORTATION

Does your school have a "No Idling Zone" for school buses and cars?
☐ Yes   ☐ No

YOUR SCHOOL AND ENERGY

	Classroom 1	Classroom 2	Classroom 3	Classroom 4	Classroom 5	Classroom 6	Main Office	Library	Auditorium	Locker Rooms	Cafeteria	Hallways	Bathrooms	Other Room
LIGHTING														
Which kinds of light bulbs are used? S Standard light bulbs C Compact fluorescent light bulbs														
Are the light fixtures kept clean?														
Does the room have dimmer switches or automatic timers for any of the lights?														
If there is no automatic timer for the lights, does the last person out of the room turn off the lights?														
ELECTRICITY														
Are computers, copy machines, and printers turned off when not in use?														
Does the room have power strips?														
HEATING AND COOLING														
Are there any desks, chairs, or other pieces of equipment blocking heating or cooling vents?														
Does the room have air conditioning?														

	Classroom 1	Classroom 2	Classroom 3	Classroom 4	Classroom 5	Classroom 6	Main Office	Library	Auditorium	Locker Rooms	Cafeteria	Hallways	Bathrooms	Other Room
What settings are the air conditioners set to when in use?														
Does the room have fans?														
Does the room have windows?														
Does the room have window shades or blinds to block out sunlight during hot days?														
Are any windows cracked or broken?														
Do the windows and doors seal tightly or do they leak air? S Seal tightly L Leak air														
Are the desks and chairs arranged to take advantage of natural light?														
WATER														
Are there any leaky drinking faucets, sink faucets, showerheads, or toilets?														
If so, where?														
Are flow restrictors used?														

SCHOOL DAYS

Once the green team has analyzed the results of the survey, you can create an action plan. What changes can be made right away—quickly and easily with little or no cost? What changes need long-term planning? The goal is to lower your school's environmental impact by saving energy, recycling, and saving water. The best way to achieve this is to get everyone in the school involved—students, teachers, principals, parents, custodians, school bus drivers—everyone. Now, get going!

4 U 2 Do—Green Patrol

Get your patrol caps on!

Set up your school's own "Green Patrol." Everyone can have a different "beat," such as:

- making sure computers are off at the end of the day;
- monitoring recycling bins to make sure they aren't being used for trash;
- turning lights or power strips off; or
- posting "Please Don't Waste Water" signs.

If recycling of cans and glass can earn money, decide on a goal.

4 U 2 Do—Living Green Fair

Help teach the whole community how to live green by organizing a *Living Green Fair* at your school.

Ask your teacher to help you organize a fun, busy evening for the whole school and community. Search for green businesses such as solar-energy companies, lighting companies, organic farmers who sell "shares" (called CSAs, or Community Supported Agriculture), local natural foods restaurants, and recycled-product suppliers.

Different teams can
- organize booths;
- do publicity with newspaper notices, posters, and so on; or
- organize games or raffles.

Your teacher can work with your school's principal to select a day or evening and a location such as the school gymnasium and auditorium. Find out if the time and location are available. Make sure it's at least two months away to allow enough time for planning. Then, write letters inviting the PTA, other schools in your school district, and local businesses to participate. There's an example on the next page.

Date

Dear _____:

Our class is organizing a Living Green Fair to help the
community learn more about how to live green and lower
our impact on Earth. The Fair will be held
on _____ at _____.

You are invited to participate by setting up a booth,
contributing to raffle prizes, etc. Please let us know if
you are interested. You can contact us at
_____.

Sincerely,

                                    's Class
Mr./Ms._____

CHAPTER 4

IT'S UP TO US!

Silently but swiftly, our planet is changing around us. As long as carbon dioxide keeps rising, temperatures will keep rising, too. It's up to us to stop global climate change. It's up to us to restore Earth's natural balance. The really great news is that we know what to do—and the solutions are catching on.

- *Switch* to clean energy to power our lives.
- *Conserve* energy in our homes, schools, and communities.
- *Make some noise* to let others know we care and to spread the word about how to keep our planet healthy.

Just like you, people all over the globe are taking action. Just like you, they are taking steps little and large to live in ways that are healthier for themselves and for our planet. Together, each of our small steps will add up to make a big difference!

GLOSSARY

ALTERNATIVE ENERGY: Energy that is not widely used and is usually environmentally friendly, like solar or wind energy (as opposed to fossil fuels).

ALTERNATIVE TRANSPORTATION: Modes of transportation other than cars, like walking, bicycling, rollerblading, carpooling, and public transportation.

BIODEGRADABLE: Made mostly of natural materials that can be broken down and used by the ecosystem. For example, cotton is biodegradable, while plastic is not.

CARBON DIOXIDE (CO_2): A naturally occurring greenhouse gas in the atmosphere. Concentrations have increased (from 280 parts per million in preindustrial times to about 385 parts per million today) as a result of human activities that burn fossil fuels (coal, oil, natural gas) and organic matter (e.g., wood).

CARBON FOOTPRINT: The amount of carbon dioxide that a person (or family) directly or indirectly adds to the air as a result of all the energy they use.

CARPOOLING: Sharing a car to reduce fuel use, pollution, and travel costs.

COMPACT FLUORESCENT LIGHT BULBS: Flourescent light bulbs small enough to fit into standard light sockets. They are much more energy-efficient than regular incandescent bulbs.

ENERGY EFFICIENCY: Technologies and methods that reduce the amount of electricity and/or fuel used to do the same work, like powering a home, office, or factory.

FOSSIL FUELS: Nonrenewable energy resources such as coal, oil, and natural gas that are formed from the compression of plant and animal remains over hundreds of millions of years.

GREEN DESIGN: Design that uses environmentally friendly principles of construction and energy use, such as solar panels, skylights, and recycled building materials.

GREENHOUSE EFFECT: The warming that occurs when certain gases (greenhouse gases) are present in a planet's atmosphere. Visible light from the Sun penetrates the atmosphere of a planet and heats the ground. The warmed ground then radiates infrared radiation back toward space. If greenhouse gases are present, they absorb some of that radiation, trapping it and making the planet warmer than it otherwise would be.

GREENHOUSE GASES: Gases such as carbon dioxide, water vapor, and methane that absorb infrared radiation. When these gases are present in a planet's atmosphere, they absorb some of the heat trying to escape the planet instead of letting it pass through the atmosphere, resulting in a greenhouse effect.

LIVING GREEN: Living in a way that lessens one's impact on the environment.

LOCAVORE: A person who consumes locally grown and produced food, usually within a 100 mile radius of where she or he lives.

PHOTOSYNTHESIS: Process by which plants use energy from sunlight to convert carbon dioxide and water into food (in the form of sugar). Oxygen is released in the process.

RECYCLING: System of collecting, sorting, and reprocessing old material into usable raw materials.

RENEWABLE ENERGY: Energy sources like wind and sunlight that produce energy indefinitely.

WASTE: Material that cannot be recycled or reused (synonymous with trash or garbage).

REFERENCES

We used a wide variety of resources in writing this book. A few, however, were especially helpful. We recommend these resources for students, educators, librarians, and parents who want to learn more about how to lessen their impact on Earth and live a greener life.

- *Climate Change 2007*, the most recent United Nations Report of the Intergovernmental Panel on Climate Change (IPCC). This *Synthesis Report* summarizes three separate reports: *The Physical Science Basis*; *Impacts, Adaptation, and Vulnerability*; and *Mitigation of Climate Change*; providing the current state of knowledge. It clearly summarizes the causes and consequences of climate change. In addition, the Frequently Asked Questions (FAQs) for *The Physical Science Basis* provides clear explanations, with illustrations, of many topics *(e.g., What Is the Relationship between Climate Change and Weather? How Are Temperatures on Earth Changing?)* **www.ipcc.ch.**

- *Dire Predictions: Understanding Global Warming* (2009) by leading climate scientists Michael E. Mann and Lee R. Kump. This book is an illustrated guide to the findings of the Intergovernmental Panel on Climate Change (IPCC). It's a wonderful book with many helpful illustrations to explain the science behind climate change.

- *The Forgiving Air: Understanding Environmental Change* (Second Edition, 2008) by Richard C. Somerville, one of the world's top climate scientists. This is a fascinating and understandable book about climate science based on a series of lectures to K12 teachers.

RESOURCES

*E*arth's Precious Resources: Clean Air by Andrew Bridges, *Clean Water* by Beth Geiger, *Clean Energy* by Laurie Goldman, *Living Green* by John Johnson, Jr. (Sally Ride Science, 2008). This series describes Earth's precious resources and the challenges we face in protecting them. Clean water, clean air, and clean sources of energy are vital to all of us.

Our Changing Climate: Ecosystems by Tam O'Shaughnessy (Sally Ride Science, 2008). This book draws on the latest scientific findings to describe what's happening to ecosystems around the world as a result of global warming. As our planet's air, water, and soil grow warmer, its wildlife hunts for new habitats when old ones become unlivable.

CLIMATE CENTRAL: Provides up-to-date information on climate change in a variety of formats including online and video. **climatecentral.org**

CONSUMER REPORTS GREENER CHOICES: Provides green ratings of products—from appliances and cars to electronics and food. You can use their search tools to get evaluations of labels on food, personal care products, household cleaners, and garden chemicals. **www.greenerchoices.org**

EDIBLE SCHOOLYARD: Tips (and a successful example) for starting an organic garden at your school or in your community. **www.edibleschoolyard.org**

GLOBAL CLIMATE CHANGE—NASA'S EYES ON THE EARTH: Provides information on our planet's vital signs such as global temperature, sea ice, sea level, and much more. **climate.jpl.nasa.gov**

MARIAN KOSHLAND SCIENCE MUSEUM: Online exhibit about global warming and our future from the National Academy of Sciences. **www.koshland-science-museum .org/exhibitgcc**

NATIONAL OCEANIC AND ATMOSPHERIC ADMINISTRATION: Provides up-to-date information on global climate change with educational resources including a photo archive of thousands of images. **www.research.noaa.gov/climate**

NATURAL RESOURCES DEFENSE COUNCIL: Provides downloadable guides with tips for buying clean energy and a hybrid car, saving gas and cutting energy use, and recycling and reducing garbage. **www.nrdc.org**

SCRIPPS CO_2 PROGRAM: Provides the history of measuring carbon dioxide in the air and gives the monthy measurements of carbon dioxide in the air from Mauna Loa, Hawaii, 1958 to present. **www.scrippsco2.ucsd.edu**

U.S. DEPARTMENT OF ENERGY: Kid's website with games, tips, and facts about saving energy. **www.eere.energy.gov/kids**

U.S. ENVIRONMENTAL PROTECTION AGENCY: Provides extensive information about how to protect the environment and ways to save money. **www.epa.gov**. Kid's website about global climate change with games, animations, and links to other resources. **www.epa .gov/globalwarming/kids/index.html**

U.S. GEOLOGICAL SURVEY: Provides activities, fun facts and cool stuff to use from satellites studying Earth in space. **terraweb.wr.usgs.gov/kids**

ABOUT THE AUTHORS

Sally Ride, best known for being the first American woman in space, is an Emerita Professor of Physics at the University of California, San Diego. Dr. Ride has B.S., M.S., and Ph.D. degrees in Physics, all from Stanford University. During eight years as a NASA astronaut, she flew on two space shuttle missions, served on the President's Commission investigating the space shuttle *Challenger* accident, and headed NASA's long-range planning after the accident. Since leaving NASA, she has committed herself to improving science education. Dr. Ride is currently President and CEO of Sally Ride Science, a K12 science education company that creates programs and publications to support students' natural interest in science, and places a special emphasis on encouraging girls.

Dr. Ride has received numerous honors and awards, and has co-authored seven children's science books, including *The Third Planet* (co-authored with Tam O'Shaughnessy), which won the American Institute of Physics Children's Science Writing Award.

Tam O'Shaughnessy has been interested in science since she was a little girl. One of her favorite childhood memories is of watching tadpoles in a creek gradually sprout legs, go green, and turn into frogs. She studied biology in college, earning B.S. and M.S. degrees from Georgia State University. While teaching college biology, she became interested in how kids learn and went on to earn her Ph.D. in school psychology from the University of California, Riverside. Dr. O'Shaughnessy is currently the COO and Executive Vice President of Sally Ride Science and a Professor Emerita of Education at San Diego State University. A former science teacher and award-winning children's science writer, she oversees the development of Sally Ride Science's classroom books, teacher guides, and educator institutes. Dr. O'Shaughnessy is the author of ten science books for children.

THIS BOOK IS DEDICATED TO OUR READERS—THE NEXT GENERATION OF SCIENTISTS, ENGINEERS, AND COMMUNITY ORGANIZERS WHO WILL COME UP WITH WAYS TO KEEP OUR PLANET HEALTHY.

WHAT'S THE BEST WAY TO FIGHT GLOBAL WARMING?
LEARN MORE ABOUT IT!

"To a person standing on the ground, our air seems to go on forever. The sky looks so big, and people haven't worried about what they put in the air. From space, though, it's obvious how little air there really is. Nothing vanishes 'into thin air.' The gases that we're sending into the air are piling up in our atmosphere. And that's changing Earth's life support system in ways that could change our planet forever."

Mission: Planet Earth is a compelling introduction to the Earth and the changes taking place in its climate, written for the audience that matters most to our planet's future: kids!

Find out how the planet's systems work: how water, air, and other climate systems shape our world, and what happens when one of them is affected.

With helpful diagrams, clear illustrations, and stunning photographs from the front lines of climate change, *Mission: Planet Earth* is a clear, even-handed, and thoughtful account of the changes that are affecting every part of our planet, from the Arctic to the deserts and from the highest peaks to the depths of the oceans.

To learn more, visit www.missionplanetearth.com.